Spices

Allspice

Black mustard

Black Pepper

Cardamom

Chili

Cinnamon

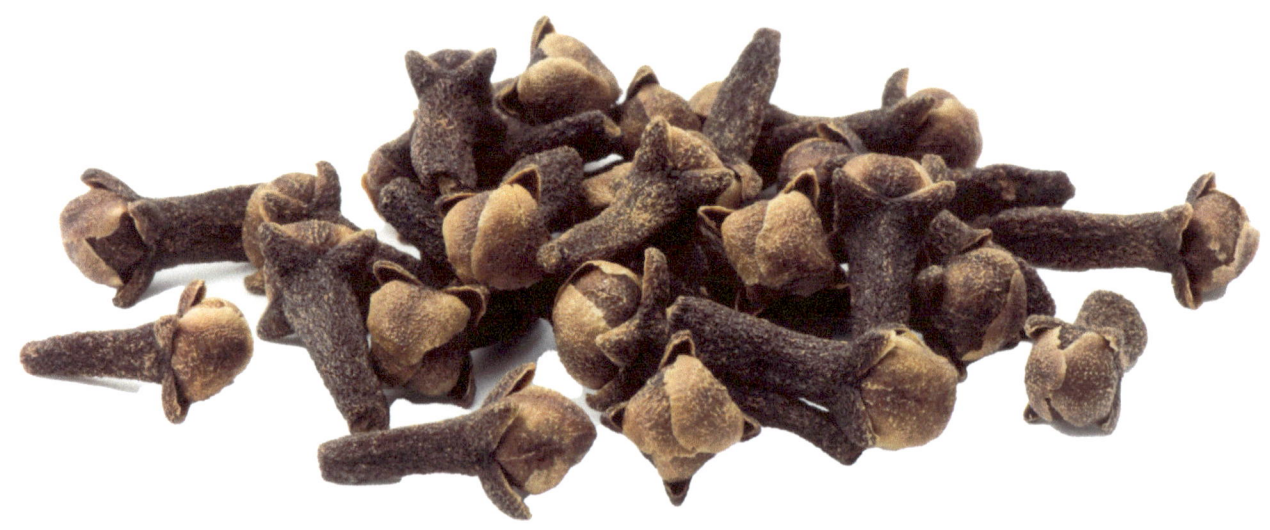

Cloves

Cumin

Dill

Fennel

Fenugreek

Garam masala

Garlic

Ginger

Nigella sativa

Nutmeg

Paprika

Saffron

Sesame

Star anise

Sumac

Turmeric

Vanilla

Yellow mustard

www.ingramcontent.com/pod-product-compliance
Lightning Source LLC
Chambersburg PA
CBHW041526070526
44585CB00002B/97